Nightmares
On the big screen

The terrifying history of horror cinema

Contents

Introduction

Definition of Horror Cinema

Horror cinema is a film genre that aims to frighten and evoke fear and anxiety in the viewer. This genre is characterized by the graphic representation of violence, terror, and the supernatural. Horror cinema relies on visual and auditory elements such as makeup, special effects, music, and sound to create a disturbing and terrifying atmosphere.

Horror cinema is often associated with themes such as death, madness, occultism, monsters, zombies, ghosts, and serial killers. It can be divided into several subgenres, each with its own distinct characteristics. Popular subgenres of horror cinema include slasher, gothic, gore, found footage, psychological horror, survival horror, and post-apocalyptic horror.

Since its inception, horror cinema has always been controversial due to its violent and morbid content, which can shock and disturb audiences. However, the genre remains popular among a wide audience and has influenced many other areas of popular culture, such as video games, music, and literature.

Horror cinema is also a genre that constantly evolves, reflecting the fears and concerns of contemporary society. Over time, the genre has evolved to include elements of popular culture, such as references to other films, satire, and dark humor.

Objectives and Challenges of the Genre

The section «Objectives and Challenges of the Genre» is a crucial introduction to understanding the significance and impact of horror cinema. The main objective of this film genre is to scare and frighten the audience by using elements of horror, suspense, and tension. Horror films are created to provoke intense sensations and emotions in viewers, who often seek unique and unforgettable experiences at the cinema.

Horror cinema also aims to reveal humanity's deepest and darkest fears, such as death, loneliness, loss of control, madness, and fear of the unknown. Horror films often explore common phobias, such as spiders, snakes, clowns, confined spaces, and darkness, in order to evoke primal emotions in the audience.

Furthermore, horror cinema can also be used to address social and political issues, such as discrimination, injustice, and violence, by reflecting them in imaginary and extreme situations. Thus, horror films can be an effective means of raising awareness about certain social issues and encouraging people to reflect on their own perception of the world around them.

One of the challenges of the genre is to constantly evolve in order to continue eliciting strong reactions from the audience. Filmmakers and screenwriters must constantly find new ideas, new approaches, and new ways of telling horror stories to keep films relevant and captivating. In addition, horror cinema must also compete with other film genres and with new technologies such as streaming platforms, which are changing the way audiences consume films.

Origins of Horror Cinema

The origins of horror cinema can be traced back to the early days of cinema, when films were primarily sensational attractions intended to shock and scare the audience. The Lumière brothers created one of the first horror films in 1896, titled «Le Manoir du Diable,» which featured a sudden appearance of a devil on the screen. This short film was a success with the public and paved the way for many other horror films.

Early horror films were often inspired by gothic literature, with stories featuring vampires, ghosts, werewolves, and monsters. Film adaptations of novels by Mary Shelley, Bram Stoker, and Edgar Allan Poe were particularly popular.

However, early horror films were often criticized for their lack of artistic quality and their simple use of violence and surprise effects to provoke reactions from the audience. The genre was not considered serious or worthy of interest for serious filmmakers.

This began to change with the arrival of silent cinema, when directors such as Georges Méliès started using special effects to create horrific and fantastic images on screen. Silent films like «The Cabinet of Dr. Caligari» (1920) and «Nosferatu» (1922) also introduced elements of German expressionism, which influenced the visual style of the genre for decades to come.

In the 1930s, major Hollywood studios began producing high-quality horror films, such as «Frankenstein» (1931) and «Dracula» (1931), with famous actors like Boris Karloff and Bela Lugosi. These films were made with significant budgets and meticulous attention to staging, art direction, and cinematography, which contributed to making horror cinema a respected genre.

In the 1960s and 1970s, horror cinema experienced a new wave of creativity, with the emergence of directors such as Roman Polanski, George A. Romero, and Dario Argento. Films from this period explored more complex themes, such as politics, sexuality, and modern society, while maintaining the characteristic horror atmosphere of the genre.

In the following decades, horror cinema continued to evolve and diversify, with the emergence of subgenres such as slasher, psychological horror, and found footage. Films like «Halloween» (1978), «The Texas Chainsaw Massacre» (1974), and «The Blair Witch Project» (1999) set milestones in the genre and inspired filmmakers around the world.

Today, horror cinema is more popular than ever, with films like «Get Out» (2017), «Hereditary» (2018), and «A Quiet Place» (2018) achieving great critical and commercial success. The genre has also been popularized by television series, including shows like «American Horror Story» and «The Walking Dead.»

Thus, the origins of horror cinema are rooted in the history of cinema itself, with films that began as sensational attractions before transforming into a respected artistic genre. Filmmakers have constantly pushed the boundaries of the genre, exploring more complex themes while preserving the characteristic horror atmosphere.

Despite initial criticism, horror cinema is now a popular and respected genre, with a significant influence on popular culture and the film industry as a whole. As a film genre, horror has evolved to reflect contemporary concerns while continuing to evoke intense emotions in viewers.

The Pioneers of Horror Cinema

Silent Film and Early Horror Movies

Horror cinema, although now a major genre in the film industry, began to take shape in the early days of cinema. Indeed, early horror films were influenced by the macabre stories and popular urban legends of the time.

The first ever horror film was «Le Manoir du Diable» (1896) by Georges Méliès. This three-minute short film depicts a sorcerer in a frightening manor, conjuring up ghosts and demons to terrorize a young woman. This piece is considered the first horror film in the history of cinema.

In the 1910s, horror cinema was primarily represented by silent short films, such as «Le Golem» (1915) by Paul Wegener or «Le Cabinet du Dr Caligari» (1920) by Robert Wiene. These films were characterized by expressionist sets and a dark and eerie atmosphere.

However, it was only with the advent of sound cinema that the horror genre truly became popular. In 1931, «Dracula» and «Frankenstein» were major commercial successes, thus establishing the foundations of classical horror cinema.

Silent film was also a stage for important technical innovations in the horror genre. Filmmakers used rudimentary special effects to create terrifying scenes, such as stop-motion animation to bring monsters or skeletons to life.

Silent film also inspired modern horror films, such as F.W. Murnau's «Nosferatu» (1922), a German silent film that has become a classic of the genre. «Nosferatu» is an unauthorized adaptation of Bram Stoker's novel «Dracula,» where the vampire is portrayed as a frightening and deformed creature with sharp teeth and claws. The character of Nosferatu has become an iconic figure in the horror genre.

Beyond its technical and aesthetic innovations, silent film also addressed recurring themes in horror cinema, such as death, the supernatural, and the fear of the unknown and the strange. The early horror filmmakers also sought to frighten the audience by exploiting humanity's deepest and most primal fears.

In summary, silent film was a laboratory of experimentation for horror cinema, where directors tried to find ways to scare the audience with primitive special effects and macabre stories. These early horror films laid the foundations for a genre that has now become a major part of the film industry.

The Great Directors and Actors of the Era

Horror cinema is a rich and complex genre that emerged over a century ago and has been shaped by many great directors and actors. These artists brought their own vision to the genre, creating iconic horror films that captivated audiences and made their mark on the history of cinema.

The origins of horror cinema are linked to the arrival of silent films, particularly Georges Méliès, the French director who made the first ever horror film, «Le Manoir du Diable» in 1896.

Over the years, many other directors followed in Méliès' footsteps, seeking to capture the imagination of audiences with stories of monsters, ghosts, and terrifying creatures. Among them are names such as F.W. Murnau, who made the German expressionist film «Nosferatu» in 1922, and James Whale, who directed «Frankenstein» in 1931.

The 1930s-1950s were the golden age of horror cinema, with directors such as Tod Browning, who directed «Dracula» in 1931, and Jacques Tourneur, who directed «Cat People» in 1942. These films laid the foundations of the genre, establishing conventions that are still used in horror films today, such as the eerie atmosphere, sound effects, and dim lighting.

The 1960s-1970s saw the emergence of a new wave of directors, such as Roman Polanski, who directed «Rosemary's Baby» in 1968, and George Romero, who directed «Night of the Living Dead» in 1968, considered the first zombie film. These directors brought a more subtle and complex vision to the genre, exploring themes such as paranoia, alienation, and loss of control.

In the 1980s-1990s, slashers and psychological horror took center stage, with directors such as Wes Craven, who directed «A Nightmare on Elm Street» in 1984, and David Cronenberg, who directed «The Fly» in 1986. These films introduced new elements to the genre, such as dark humor, irony, and visceral horror.

From the 2000s to the present, there has been a resurgence of the genre with directors such as James Wan, who directed «Saw» in 2004, and Jordan Peele, who directed «Get Out» in 2017. These filmmakers have brought a more original and innovative vision to the genre, combining elements of horror cinema with social and political themes.

In addition to directors, many actors have also made their mark on the genre, bringing their talent and charisma to horror films. Bela Lugosi, for example, played the role of Dracula in the 1931 film, bringing a hypnotic and unsettling presence to the character. Similarly, Boris Karloff played the role of Frankenstein's monster in the 1931 film, adding a touch of empathy to a character that could have been a mere monster.

Other actors have also left their mark on the genre, such as Vincent Price, who appeared in several horror films in the 1960s-1970s, bringing elegance and biting irony to his roles. Jamie Lee Curtis, on the other hand, starred in «Halloween» in 1978, launching her career as an actress and becoming an icon of horror cinema.

In addition to directors and actors, it is worth mentioning the screenwriters and composers who have helped shape the genre. Names such as Richard Matheson, who wrote «I Am Legend,» brought psychological and emotional depth to horror stories, while composers such as Bernard Herrmann created unforgettable scores that contributed to enhancing the atmosphere of tension and terror in films.

Literary Adaptations

Literary adaptations have always been a source of inspiration for horror cinema. From the early days of cinema, directors have sought to adapt terrifying stories for the big screen. These literary adaptations have allowed horror writers to reach a wider audience and have provided horror cinema with stories rich in detail, complex characters, and captivating plots.

One of the most impactful literary adaptations in horror cinema is undoubtedly Bram Stoker's «Dracula,» first adapted in 1931 by Tod Browning. The film features Bela Lugosi in the role of Count Dracula, who has become an icon of horror cinema and has inspired numerous subsequent adaptations. Stoker's novel, originally published in 1897, is a gothic epistolary tale that explores the fear of the unknown, death, and sexuality. Browning's film preserved the essence of the novel while also adding striking visual elements, such as the dark and eerie set of the Count's castle.

Another successful adaptation of a horror novel is Mary Shelley's «Frankenstein,» which was first adapted in 1931 by James Whale. The film features Boris Karloff in the role of the monster created by Dr. Frankenstein. Like «Dracula,» Whale's film remained faithful to the essence of Shelley's novel while adding a visual and dramatic dimension. Shelley's novel, published in 1818, is a gothic narrative about man's boundless ambition and the consequences of creating life. Whale's film emphasized the tragic aspect of the character of the monster, who is rejected by society and desperately seeks meaning in his life.

Literary adaptations have also allowed horror cinema to explore new horizons. Science fiction novels, such as Jack Finney's «Invasion of the Body Snatchers,» have been adapted into suspenseful horror films, while popular tales, such as «Little Red Riding Hood,» have been transformed into bloody horror stories like John Landis's «An American Werewolf in London.»

However, not all literary adaptations are created equal. Some are faithful to the spirit and tone of the original work, while others take liberties with the plot and characters. Some adaptations can even surpass the original work, such as William Friedkin's «The Exorcist,» which is considered one of the greatest horror films of all time, even though William Peter Blatty's novel is also acclaimed.

Literary adaptations continue to be a source of inspiration for today's horror cinema. The novels of Stephen King, one of the best-known and most popular horror writers, have been successfully adapted into films such as «The Shining,» «It,» and «Pet Sematary.» The adaptations of King's works have often succeeded in capturing the psychological horror present in his novels. The film adaptations of King's works have also helped popularize horror cinema among a younger audience who discovered the author through films like «It.»

Other horror authors have also seen their works successfully adapted into horror films, such as H.P. Lovecraft, who is often considered one of the most influential writers in the horror genre. Film adaptations of Lovecraft's works, such as «Re-Animator» and «From Beyond,» have managed to capture the dark and oppressive atmosphere that characterizes his writings.

Literary adaptations have also allowed horror cinema to develop a unique and recognizable aesthetic. Filmmakers have often sought to recreate the images and atmospheres described in novels while adding visual elements such as lighting and sets to enhance horror and suspense. Literary adaptations have also allowed filmmakers to create memorable characters, such as Frankenstein's monster or Count Dracula, who have become cultural icons.

Iconic Films and Their Cultural Impact

The section on iconic horror films is undoubtedly one of the most exciting and historically rich parts of this cinematic art form. Horror films have always had a significant cultural impact, influencing not only subsequent films but also popular culture in general.

As a horror cinema enthusiast, it is important to mention the films that have shaped the genre, opened new doors, and inspired a generation of filmmakers. We can begin with Alfred Hitchcock's «Psycho» in 1960. Considered one of the most influential films of all time, «Psycho» revolutionized the horror genre by introducing elements of suspense and psychological terror. This film is also known for its famous shower scene, which has become one of the most iconic scenes in the history of cinema. The success of «Psycho» paved the way for a new wave of horror films that explored darker and deeper themes.

Another film that had a significant cultural impact is George A. Romero's «Night of the Living Dead» in 1968. This film popularized the zombie film genre and influenced many other filmmakers. Romero was also praised for his exploration of social and political themes, including racial tensions and the Vietnam War.

William Friedkin's «The Exorcist» in 1973 is another iconic horror film that had a significant cultural impact. The film introduced the theme of demonic possession and was praised for its realistic and shocking depiction of exorcism. It was also controversial due to its graphic violence and blasphemous content.

John Carpenter's «Halloween» in 1978 popularized the slasher genre, featuring a serial killer who stalks and kills his victims in a violent manner. This film created the iconic character of Michael Myers and was followed by numerous sequels and remakes. The film also influenced other directors and created a distinct subgenre within horror cinema.

Wes Craven's «A Nightmare on Elm Street» in 1984 is another iconic film that had a significant cultural impact. This film popularized the character of Freddy Krueger, a serial killer who haunts his victims in their dreams. The film introduced elements of dark comedy into the horror genre and influenced many other films and television series.

Finally, Jonathan Demme's «The Silence of the Lambs» in 1991 is another iconic horror film that was praised for its outstanding performances and captivating screenplay. This film popularized the intelligent and charismatic serial killer character and influenced many other films and television series. It was also the first horror film to win the Academy Award for Best Picture, elevating the genre to the status of art.

These iconic films all had a significant cultural impact and influenced many other horror films that followed. They also demonstrated that horror can be used to explore deep and universal themes. These films also inspired a generation of filmmakers who sought to push the boundaries of the genre and explore new narrative and aesthetic paths. Horror remains an important and influential genre in the world of cinema, and these iconic films remain references for filmmakers and fans of the genre.

The Evolution of the Genre

1930s-1950s: The Golden Age of Horror Cinema

The years from the 1930s to the 1950s were a heyday for horror cinema, and for good reason. The first films of the genre had already been produced in the 1920s, with F.W. Murnau's classic «Nosferatu» released in 1922. However, it was in the 1930s that the genre truly exploded, with the emergence of numerous masterpieces that would influence the genre for decades to come. This period is often considered the golden age of horror cinema, as it saw the rise of many great directors and actors, as well as advancements in film technology that allowed for significant progress in special effects and the creation of horrifying atmospheres.

Among the early successes of this period were Universal Pictures' «Dracula» and «Frankenstein.» Tod Browning's «Dracula,» released in 1931 and starring Bela Lugosi in the lead role, marked the advent of a horror icon, the vampire, and laid the foundations for the gothic genre, which would continue to influence horror cinema for decades. James Whale's «Frankenstein,» also released in the same year, was praised for its performances, gothic set designs, and poignant storyline. The film was also lauded for its ability to evoke empathy towards Frankenstein's creature, portrayed by Boris Karloff, despite his monstrous appearance.

These two films marked the beginning of the golden age of horror cinema. The years that followed witnessed the emergence of other classics, such as George Waggner's

«The Wolf Man» in 1941, which was the first film to feature a complete visual transformation of man into a wolf. This film was a considerable success, thanks in part to Lon Chaney Jr.'s performance, which brought emotional depth to his tormented character.

The 1930s-1950s also saw the emergence of specific subgenres, such as mummy films, with Karl Freund's «The Mummy» in 1932, starring Boris Karloff. The film was praised for its performances, gothic set designs, and ominous atmosphere, and inspired numerous similar films in the years that followed.

In addition to monster films, this period also saw the emergence of great horror directors and actors, such as James Whale, Tod Browning, Boris Karloff, Bela Lugosi, Vincent Price, and Christopher Lee. These talents continued to work within the genre and contributed to its popularity and influence in the decades to come.

Finally, the years from the 1930s to the 1950s were also marked by the use of technology to achieve spectacular special effects, particularly in monster films such as «King Kong» in 1933 and «The Creature from the Black Lagoon» in 1949. Technological advancements allowed for the creation of eerie atmospheres, as seen in Ernest B. Schoedsack's «The Most Dangerous Game» in 1932, where the creation of a dense and menacing jungle environment contributed to the film's sense of horror.

In addition to these technical advancements, the 1930s-1950s also witnessed the emergence of more sophisticated special effects, such as rubber masks, animated dolls, and detailed models. These tools allowed horror filmmakers to create more realistic and frightening monsters, immersing audiences in the world of horror.

Furthermore, the golden age of horror cinema was also marked by the rise of censorship and regulations, which began to affect the production of horror films as early as the 1930s. The Production Code Administration (PCA) was established in 1930 to regulate film production and establish standards of decency, forbidding scenes of explicit violence and sex. This forced filmmakers to rely on suggestive effects rather than directly showing the most horrifying acts, paradoxically enhancing the tension and horrific atmosphere.

1960s-1970s: The New Wave of Horror Cinema

The 1960s and 1970s were a crucial period in the history of horror cinema, witnessing the emergence of a new wave of talented and innovative directors. This period saw the arrival of styles and subgenres of horror films that would leave a lasting mark on the genre and inspire generations of future filmmakers.

The French New Wave, which began in the 1950s and extended into the early 1960s, had a major influence on horror cinema. New Wave directors, such as François Truffaut, Jean-Luc Godard, and Claude Chabrol, introduced new storytelling techniques and mise-en-scène in their films, which also found their way into the horror genre. This period saw the emergence of horror films such as Georges

Franju's «Eyes Without a Face» in 1960, which introduced gothic aesthetics to horror and created a dark and gloomy atmosphere through the use of lighting and cinematography.

The 1960s also saw the emergence of British directors who created classic horror films such as Michael Powell's «Peeping Tom» in 1960 and Jack Clayton's «The Innocents» in 1961. These films explored themes of psychology, anxiety, and sexuality, redefining the genre and attracting a more mature audience for horror cinema.

In the 1970s, horror cinema underwent a radical transformation with the arrival of a new generation of American directors who pushed the boundaries of the genre by exploring darker and more disturbing themes. Filmmakers such as George A. Romero, Wes Craven, and Tobe Hooper created films that would forever leave their mark on the genre. Romero's «Night of the Living Dead» in 1968 was a pioneer in the use of graphic violence, social satire, and politics in horror, creating the subgenre of zombie films.

In the 1970s, horror films also explored themes of childhood trauma, fear of the unknown, and urban violence. Tobe Hooper's «The Texas Chainsaw Massacre» in 1974 introduced the concept of the slasher film and established the genre's codes, such as the use of gore, an eerie soundtrack, and an oppressive atmosphere. William Friedkin's «The Exorcist» in 1973 also shocked audiences with its exploration of demonic possession and innovative special effects that created unforgettable horror sequences.

Moreover, the 1970s saw a period of great creativity in Italian horror cinema, with the emergence of the «giallo» subgenre. Giallo films introduced elements of suspense, violent murders, and sophisticated visuals, with directors such as Dario Argento and Mario Bava. Giallo films became famous for their use of colorful lighting, unusual camera angles, and avant-garde soundtracks to create a unique and distinctive atmosphere.

Beyond Europe and the United States, Asian filmmakers also began to create innovative horror films. Japan, in particular, produced many films that influenced the genre as a whole. Films such as Kaneto Shindô's «Onibaba» in 1964 introduced elements of Japanese folklore to the genre, while films such as Masaki Kobayashi's «Kwaidan» in 1964 created eerie atmospheres and ghost stories. J-horror films, such as Hideo Nakata's «Ringu» in 1998, were also influenced by these classic horror films and created their own unique style of horror.

2000s to the Present: The Revival of the Genre

The 2000s marked a spectacular revival for horror cinema, with films that revitalized the genre by exploring new territories, innovating aesthetically, and pushing the boundaries of cinematic terror.

One of the most iconic films of this period is «The Ring» (2002), an American remake of the Japanese film «Ringu» (1998). Directed by Gore Verbinski, the film breathed new life into the genre by using a sleek and minimalist aesthetic, creating intense psychological tension, and offering an intriguing and terrifying storyline. It also popularized the theme of a curse through a cursed videotape that condemns anyone who watches it to certain death.

Other notable films from this era include «Saw» (2004) directed by James Wan, which popularized the torture porn subgenre, and «Hostel» (2005) directed by Eli Roth, which was praised for its treatment of macabre tourism. These films sparked debates about violence and torture on screen but also showed that horror cinema could be an innovative and thought-provoking force in the film landscape.

The 2000s also witnessed the emergence of found footage, a filmmaking style that imitates the aesthetics of surveillance footage or amateur documentary. The film «The Blair Witch Project» (1999) was one of the pioneers of the genre, but it was «Paranormal Activity» (2007) that popularized the style with its realistic portrayal of a haunted house. Other films such as «Cloverfield» (2008) and «REC» (2007) also used found footage to create an immersive and terrifying cinematic experience.

Finally, the 2000s saw a number of films that explored themes of apocalypse, post-apocalyptic scenarios, and survival horror. Films such as «28 Days Later» (2002), «The Mist» (2007), and «The Road» (2009) depicted dark and nightmarish visions of humanity's future, often through characters facing unimaginable horrors and heartbreaking choices.

In summary, the 2000s were a rich and fertile period for horror cinema, with films that explored new territories and classic themes using innovative approaches and ingenious visual techniques. This period proved that horror cinema could be a fertile ground for experimentation and creativity while offering audiences unforgettable thrills and lasting nightmares.

Subgenres and Recurring Themes

Gothic and Eerie Atmosphere

The gothic theme and eerie atmosphere are two elements that have considerable significance in the horror genre. The origin of this theme is often attributed to Mary Shelley's literary work, Frankenstein; or, The Modern Prometheus, published in 1818. This novel depicts a mad scientist who, in his desire to defy the laws of nature, creates a monstrous being, which is considered the first incarnation of Frankenstein's monster. This work sparked a fascination with the macabre and the supernatural, which has influenced many artists, including horror film directors.

Horror films have used the gothic theme to create dark, distressing, and oppressive atmospheres. This ambiance is often created through gothic sets, haunted castles, cemeteries, catacombs, abandoned churches, and isolated villages. Visual elements such as lit candles, cobwebs, tombstones, and broken crucifixes are also used to reinforce the atmosphere.

The use of color is also important in creating an eerie ambiance. Horror films often employ a palette of dark and cold colors, such as blue, gray, and black. This use of colors creates a disturbing atmosphere that enhances the sense of danger and threat.

In addition to creating a gothic and eerie atmosphere, the gothic theme is often associated with iconic characters such as vampires, werewolves, ghosts, and mummies. These characters are often linked to stories of tragedy and curses, which amplify the dramatic aspect of the theme.

The gothic theme experienced a resurgence in the 1960s and 1970s with the popularity of Hammer Film Productions, a British production company specializing in horror films. These films often featured gothic sets and classic characters from gothic literature, such as Dracula, Frankenstein, the Werewolf, and the Mummy. The Hammer films also introduced a dose of violence and eroticism to the genre, renewing audience interest in horror cinema.

Today, the gothic theme remains an important element of the horror genre, although filmmakers often use modern variations of the genre. Contemporary horror films often incorporate gothic elements, such as ancient settings and iconic characters, but frequently combine them with modern elements such as cutting-edge technology and social media.

Gore and Visceral Horror

Gore and visceral horror are popular subgenres of the horror genre, known for their graphic representation of violence, mutilation, and murder. Bloody scenes and shocking images are often used to provoke strong emotional reactions from the audience, creating an intense and immersive atmosphere.

The term «gore» first appeared in the 1960s-1970s to describe films such as Herschell Gordon Lewis's «Blood Feast» (1963) and «Two Thousand Maniacs!» (1964). These films featured scenes of extreme violence and mutilation, and gave rise to a new cinematic genre that would inspire many horror film directors.

Gore is often associated with a bloody aesthetic that uses special effects and makeup to create impressive and often realistic visual effects. This aesthetic is characteristic of «splatter» films, a subgenre of gore that highlights special effects and graphic violence. «Splatter» films are often considered the most extreme and violent of the genre.

Visceral horror, on the other hand, portrays strong and often repulsive images that seek to provoke intense emotional reactions from the viewer. Visceral horror films are often characterized by a brutal and realistic aesthetic that may include images of mutilated corpses, blood, and guts.

Gore and visceral horror have often been criticized for their graphic and violent nature. Some critics have accused the genre of glorifying violence and being morally reprehensible. However, others have defended the genre, claiming that these films merely reflect the violence of contemporary society and provide a space for catharsis for the audience.

The genre has also influenced other forms of art, including video games and comic books. Combat video games such as «Mortal Kombat» have been inspired by gore and visceral horror, and horror comics such as «The Walking Dead» have popularized the genre among a broader audience.

Despite the controversy surrounding the genre, gore

and visceral horror continue to be popular among horror enthusiasts. Films such as «Saw» (2004) and «Hostel» (2005) have achieved commercial success, while directors such as Quentin Tarantino and Robert Rodriguez have incorporated elements of gore into their work.

Monster and Creature Films

Monster and creature films are an exciting and popular subgenre of the horror genre. This subgenre focuses on frightening creatures, often fantastical or imaginary, that aim to scare the audience. Monster and creature films can draw inspiration from science fiction, fantasy, mythology, or folklore.

Monsters and creatures can take many forms in horror films. They can be mutant animals, extraterrestrials, zombies, vampires, werewolves, ghosts, or even imaginary creatures like Bigfoot or Frankenstein's monster. Monster and creature films are often associated with spectacular special effects that contribute to creating an atmosphere of terror and suspense. Creatures can be brought to life through costumes and prosthetics, post-production special effects, or even 3D animation. Sound effects and music also contribute to creating an atmosphere of terror and suspense.

Monster and creature films have been popular since the early days of horror cinema. Classics such as King Kong (1933) and Godzilla (1954) were box office successes and inspired numerous sequels and remakes. Monster and creature films can also include elements of science fiction, such as the films in the Alien series (1979) or the Jurassic Park franchise (1993), which feature fantastic and terrifying creatures.

Other notable films include The Blue Lagoon (1949), The Birds (1963), The Fly (1986), and Tremors (1990). In these films, creatures are often portrayed as enemies who threaten human characters, creating dramatic tension and intense suspense.

Monster and creature films also lend themselves to adaptations of popular novels and comic books. For example, Steven Spielberg's Jaws (1975) is based on Peter Benchley's novel, while Tim Burton's Batman (1989) is an adaptation of Bob Kane's comic book.

Monster and creature films have also inspired toys, video games, books, and comics. Franchises such as Godzilla, Jurassic Park, and Alien have created popular merchandise and influenced popular culture.

Ultimately, monster and creature films play an important role in the history of the horror genre. These films have captivated audiences with frightening creatures, impressive special effects, and imaginative storytelling. They have also inspired many directors to create original and innovative horror films. Monster and creature films are an essential subgenre of horror cinema and continue to thrill audiences worldwide.

Zombie and Invasion Films

The theme of zombies and invasions is one of the most iconic and popular subgenres of the horror genre. Zombie and invasion films are characterized by situations in which a crowd of people, once human, transform into undead or monstrous creatures and invade a city, a country, or even the entire planet. In this section, we will explore the origins, themes, and techniques of zombie and invasion films, as well as their impact on popular culture.

The origins of zombie films can be traced back to Haitian voodoo culture, where zombies were people brought back to life by a sorcerer. The first zombie films, such as White Zombie (1932) and I Walked with a Zombie (1943), were influenced by this culture. However, it was not until the 1960s that director George A. Romero revolutionized the genre with his film Night of the Living Dead (1968), which introduced flesh-eating undead for the first time. This film paved the way for many other zombie films, such as Dawn of the Dead (1978), 28 Days Later (2002), and World War Z (2013).

Invasion films, on the other hand, have often been influenced by fears of the Cold War and nuclear apocalypse. Films such as The War of the Worlds (1953) and Invasion of the Body Snatchers (1956) presented extraterrestrial invaders, while others, such as The Day the Earth Stood Still (1951) and The Andromeda Strain (1971), portrayed the consequences of technology on humanity. More recently, films such as Independence Day (1996) and War of the Worlds (2005) have depicted large-scale alien invasions.

Zombie and invasion films often delve into deeper themes such as the fear of death, isolation, madness, and the destruction of society. Zombie films, in particular, have frequently been used to explore political and social themes such as racism and government corruption. The film Night of the Living Dead, for instance, featured a black protagonist, which was a bold and revolutionary decision at the time.

Technically, zombie and invasion films are often characterized by epic battle scenes, bloody special effects, and terrifying makeup. Chaotic crowd scenes are common in both genres, and many films have been made on a limited budget, leading to creative use of camera and set design. Invasion films often employ special effects to depict extraterrestrial invaders and their spacecraft, while zombie films often use special effects to show the transformation of humans into the undead.

Finally, zombie and invasion films have had a significant impact on popular culture. Zombies, in particular, have become a phenomenon in popular culture with successful television series like The Walking Dead, video games like Resident Evil, and novels such as World War Z by Max Brooks. Invasion films, in turn, have inspired video games like XCOM and television series such as Falling Skies.

Paranormal and Ghost Stories

The section on the paranormal and ghost stories in horror cinema is an important component of the genre that has captivated audiences for decades. Ghost stories have a long history as a literary form, but it is in horror cinema that the theme has truly taken off.

Ghost stories have been a source of fascination for human beings since the dawn of civilization. In horror cinema, ghost stories have developed into a distinct and prolific subgenre that evokes a wide range of emotional reactions from viewers. The popularity of this subgenre is partly due to the ability of ghost stories to explore profound themes such as grief, loss, and regret.

Ghost stories are often associated with haunted locations, such as houses or castles where tragic events have occurred. These places are often presented as sites of trauma that have left a residual emotional imprint, experienced as a supernatural presence. The main characters in these films are often individuals who seek to confront tragic events from their past, which come back to haunt them in the form of ghosts. Alejandro Amenábar's film «The Others» is a notable example of this approach.

The theme of ghost stories in horror cinema is known for its skillful use of tension and suspense. Filmmakers often create scary scenes by employing camera tricks, such as close-ups, rapid camera movements, and sudden cuts. Ghost stories draw their power from the fear of the unknown, anticipation, and suggestion rather than violence and gore.

Classical films such as «The Haunting» and «The Innocents» were known for their use of suggestion and mystery, while more recent films like «The Conjuring» and «Insidious» rely on visual and sound effects to create chilling scenes. Ghost stories in horror cinema are also known for their use of music, which can play a crucial role in building atmosphere and suspense. Subtle musical compositions can intensify the sense of tension, while stronger and more dramatic notes can accompany moments of revelation or pure fear.

The theme of ghost stories in horror cinema has undergone significant evolutions over the years. Classical films were known for their use of suggestion and mystery, while more recent films have relied on visual and sound effects to create scary scenes. However, despite these differences, all ghost stories share a common element: the belief that something supernatural is at work and that characters must confront it.

Indeed, ghost stories in horror cinema can be seen as a metaphor for our deepest fears, our apprehensions of the unknown, and our struggle to understand our place in the world. Ghosts can represent events from the past that continue to haunt characters, hidden secrets, or repressed emotions. They can also symbolize supernatural forces that surpass our understanding and control, leaving us vulnerable and frightened.

Survival Horror and Post-Apocalyptic Horror

Survival horror and post-apocalyptic horror are two exciting and increasingly popular subgenres in the world of horror cinema. They allow for exploring themes such as survival, the struggle for life, and facing the unknown in extreme situations. These subgenres also hold interest in exploring the consequences of societal collapse and the struggle for survival in a world where social and moral norms have been disrupted.

Survival horror is a subgenre that emphasizes survival in extreme situations, usually caused by unforeseen events such as an epidemic, a natural disaster, or an invasion of supernatural creatures. The characters are faced with harsh living conditions and must confront dangerous and unpredictable enemies to stay alive. Survival horror films create a stressful and immersive atmosphere through cinematic techniques such as dark and desaturated sets, anxiety-inducing sound effects, and skillful camera angles.

On the other hand, post-apocalyptic horror focuses on the aftermath of a catastrophic event, such as nuclear war, a pandemic, or an ecological disaster, which has destroyed society as we know it. The characters face survival situations in a world where resources are limited and social relationships are disrupted. Post-apocalyptic horror films explore themes such as loneliness, paranoia, fear of the unknown, and the confrontation with others.

Recurring themes in these subgenres include loneliness, paranoia, fear of the unknown and of others, the quest for food and water, survival against natural elements, as well as confronting dangerous and unpredictable enemies. Survival horror and post-apocalyptic horror films often present characters with difficult moral choices while they struggle for survival.

These subgenres are also related to other genres such as science fiction, thriller, and action films. Zombie films, for example, are often a mix of survival horror and action films, while post-apocalyptic films may include elements of science fiction or dystopia.

In terms of cinematic techniques, survival horror and post-apocalyptic horror films often use dark and desaturated imagery, abandoned settings, and stress-inducing sound effects to immerse the viewer in a hostile and terrifying world. Narrative tension is also enhanced through camera choices and editing that heighten fear and anxiety.

Overall, survival horror and post-apocalyptic horror are subgenres of horror cinema that offer a unique perspective on survival and the struggle for life in extreme situations. They allow for exploring deep and universal themes such as human nature, solidarity, fear, and resilience. Furthermore, these subgenres have contributed to the evolution of the horror genre by providing new perspectives and pushing the boundaries of imagination.

Psychological Horror Films and Thrillers

Psychological horror films and thrillers are subgenres of the horror genre that have captivated audiences' attention for decades. These films use subtle tactics to provoke intense emotional tension in the viewer, creating a captivating and memorable cinematic experience.

Psychological thrillers focus on internal conflicts within characters rather than supernatural or physical horror elements. Films in this genre play on viewers' deep fears by using situations or characters that challenge their own reality. Psychological thrillers often feature complex plots and ambiguous characters, adding an extra dimension to the psychological tension.

One of the most iconic examples of a psychological thriller is Alfred Hitchcock's film «Psycho» (1960). The film tells the story of Marion Crane, an office worker who steals money and seeks refuge in an isolated motel run by Norman Bates, a disturbed young man. The film uses a complex plot and unconventional storytelling to create intense psychological tension that culminates in a memorable shower scene.

Psychological horror films, on the other hand, focus on viewers' deep fears and anxieties rather than supernatural elements. Films in this genre often employ situations or characters that appear normal and familiar but hide dark and terrifying aspects. Psychological horror films may use plot elements to prompt viewers to reflect on their own fears and anxieties.

One of the most well-known examples of a psychological horror film is Stanley Kubrick's «The Shining» (1980). The film tells the story of Jack Torrance, a struggling writer who takes a job as the winter caretaker of an isolated hotel with his family. The film uses isolation, madness, and fear of the unknown to create intense psychological tension.

Psychological horror films and thrillers often employ complex cinematic techniques to create emotional tension in the viewer. Directing, editing, music, and acting are all key elements in establishing the right atmosphere. Directors of these films may use close camera shots, abrupt transitions, and dark soundtracks to create an unsettling and terrifying ambiance.

However, psychological horror films and thrillers go beyond mere cinematic techniques. They also explore profound themes such as madness, paranoia, loss of control, the duality of human nature, and mental manipulation, among others. By using these themes, directors can provoke introspection in the viewers and prompt them to question their own reality.

The psychological thriller film «The Silence of the Lambs» (1991) directed by Jonathan Demme is a striking example of a film that explores profound themes. The film follows the investigation of Clarice Starling, a young FBI agent, as she tracks down a cannibalistic serial killer, Hannibal Lecter, who also happens to be a brilliant psychiatrist. The film addresses themes such as the duality of human nature, empathy, mental manipulation, violence, and sexuality, creating psychological tension that goes beyond the plot.

Psychological horror films and thrillers can also explore contemporary social and political subjects. Jordan Peele's film «Get Out» (2017) is a striking example of a psychological horror film that addresses issues of race and racism. The film follows the story of Chris, a young African-American man, who visits his white girlfriend's parents for a weekend. He begins to uncover terrifying secrets about his in-laws, who are engaged in surgical experiments to transfer white brains into black bodies. The film uses complex storytelling and subversive metaphors to explore issues of racial discrimination and white privilege.

Psychological horror films and thrillers have also influenced other forms of art and popular culture. Television series like David Lynch's «Twin Peaks,» Charlie Brooker's «Black Mirror,» or Bryan Fuller's «Hannibal» have all employed elements of psychological horror and thriller to captivate their audiences. Additionally, novels and comic books have also been influenced by these cinematic genres, in works such as René Barjavel's «La Nuit des temps,» Thomas Harris's «The Silence of the Lambs,» or Alan Moore's «Watchmen.»

Finally, psychological horror films and thrillers have experienced a significant resurgence in recent years thanks to the emergence of new directors and technologies. Films such as Ari Aster's «Hereditary,» Jordan Peele's «Get Out,» «Us,» also by Jordan Peele, Ari Aster's «Midsommar,» Darren Aronofsky's «Mother!,» or David Fincher's «Gone Girl» have all been praised for their ability to explore profound themes while creating intense psychological tension.

Techniques and Aesthetics of Horror Cinema

Directing and Art Direction

Directing and art direction are crucial elements for the success of a horror film. Their role is to create a chilling atmosphere and a frightening aesthetic that immerses the viewer in the film's universe. To achieve this, horror directors employ specific techniques that vary depending on the sub-genres and themes addressed.

Directing involves how the director organizes the space, movements, and camera angles in the scenes. In horror films, directing is often characterized by close-ups, subtle camera movements, unsettling camera angles, and clever use of light and darkness. For example, a slow and steady camera movement following a character walking down a dark hallway can evoke a sense of tension and apprehension among viewers.

Art direction, on the other hand, is responsible for the visual aspect of the film, such as sets, costumes, makeup, and special effects. Horror films often play with the aesthetic of horror to create a macabre and frightening ambiance. Dark colors, gloomy sets, terrifying costumes, special effects, and frightening makeup are all elements that contribute to the chilling atmosphere of a horror film. For instance, special effects can be used to create gruesome death scenes or bring terrifying creatures to life.

In addition to directing and art direction, sound design is also a key element in creating the atmosphere of a horror film. Eerie sounds, ominous music, and oppressive silence can all contribute to building palpable tension. For example, haunting music can be used to underscore a scary scene or a moment of suspense, while silence can be used to create a surprise effect.

Directing and art direction are also responsible for creating memorable and frightening characters. Monsters, serial killers, and ghosts are examples of characters that can scare audiences. To make these characters credible, horror directors must give them a terrifying appearance, as well as a personality and a backstory that make them believable.

Finally, it is important to note that directing and art direction can vary significantly depending on the sub-genres and themes being explored. Gothic horror films, for example, often focus on the use of dark sets and elegant costumes to create a gothic and romantic ambiance. Zombie films, on the other hand, may emphasize the use of makeup and special effects to create terrifying and decaying zombies.

Similarly, psychological horror and thriller sub-genres focus more on the use of narrative tension and the psychology of characters rather than visual effects. In these films, directing may use close-up shots to highlight facial expressions and emotions, or wide shots to show characters in an isolated and oppressive environment.

Photography and Lighting

Photography and lighting are essential elements in creating a horror atmosphere in horror cinema. How a scene is lit can significantly affect how the audience perceives it and can evoke a range of emotions, from fear to unease. Horror filmmakers often employ a variety of techniques to create striking and terrifying visual effects.

One common technique used in horror cinema is the play of shadow and light. Shadows are often used to create a chilling and oppressive atmosphere, particularly in horror and suspense scenes. Light sources are often positioned to highlight the most frightening features of a character or location, such as a dark and menacing figure in a dense and obscure forest.

The choice of colors used in a film is also important for the final effect. Warm and vibrant colors, such as red and orange, are often used to symbolize violence and terror, while cold and dark colors, such as blue and green, are often used to create an eerie and macabre atmosphere. Colors can also be used to differentiate characters and themes, for example by associating a specific color with a terrifying character or situation.

Furthermore, the use of different camera angles and shots can also affect the audience's perception of horror in a film. Close-up shots can create tension and intimacy that can be very frightening, while wide shots can provide an overview of a horrifying situation.

In summary, photography and lighting are key elements in creating the necessary atmosphere and tension for a successful horror film. Horror directors use a variety of techniques to create terrifying visual effects that can elicit intense emotions from the audience. The use of shadow and light, colors, camera angles and shots, and other visual techniques can help create a frightening and memorable experience for viewers.

Special Effects and Makeup

Special effects and makeup have always been key elements in horror cinema, allowing filmmakers to create terrifying scenes and credible monsters to immerse the audience in a horrific world. Since the early silent horror films, special effects have been used to evoke strong emotions from viewers. Technological advancements have allowed horror directors to push the boundaries of special effects and create increasingly immersive and frightening films.

Special effects can be divided into two categories: practical effects and visual effects. Practical effects are created on set using makeup, prosthetics, and props. Visual effects, on the other hand, are created in post-production using computers and specialized software.

Makeup is one of the most important elements of practical effects in horror. Horror makeup artists are often talented artists who have the ability to transform actors into frightening monsters. They use advanced makeup techniques, such as casting, latex, and silicone, to create prosthetics that can be applied to actors' faces.

Makeup artists can also use special effects, such as special contact lenses, to create monstrous eyes, and silicone teeth to create terrifying jaws. Wounds and scars can also be created using makeup, fake blood, and props.

Practical effects are also used to create fantastic creatures and monsters for horror films. Makeup artists often use sculptures and models to create three-dimensional models of creatures, which are then used to create molds for latex or silicone prosthetics. Makeup artists can also use accessories such as wings or tails to complete a character's look.

Visual effects are also crucial for horror cinema. Visual effects allow the creation of special effects that would be impossible to achieve using practical effects alone. Visual effects can be used to add elements such as explosions, fantastic creatures, and scary landscapes to a scene.

Visual effects can also be used to enhance practical effects. For example, visual effects can be used to add smoke or mist to a scene, or to alter the color or texture of prosthetics.

It is important to emphasize that special effects and makeup are used not only to create scary monsters and creatures but also to create an eerie atmosphere in the film. Makeup artists and special effects specialists work closely with directors to ensure that visual and practical effects align with the vision of the story and characters.

Special effects and makeup are also used to create gore and blood effects in horror films. Makeup artists can use materials such as fake blood, latex guts, and severed limbs to create graphic and bloody violence scenes.

The work of makeup artists and special effects specialists is often overlooked by the general public, but their contribution is essential to the creation of a successful horror film. Horror directors often rely on specialized effects teams to bring their terrifying visions to life.

Furthermore, technological advancements have allowed horror directors to create more advanced and realistic special effects using specialized computers and software. Visual effects can be used to create fantastic creatures and terrifying landscapes, as well as enhance practical effects.

However, despite the growing use of visual effects, many horror directors continue to favor practical effects to create believable and immersive monsters and horror scenes. Practical effects allow actors to react to tangible objects and creatures, which can enhance the quality of performances and heighten the emotions felt by the audience.

Sound and Music

Music and sound play a crucial role in horror cinema. They are key elements in creating atmosphere, eliciting emotions, and enhancing the impact of images on screen. Music can be used to create memorable themes for characters or scenes. It can also be used to create contrast between a calm scene and a terrifying one. Similarly, sound effects can bring monsters and creatures to life or amplify tension in suspenseful moments.

In early horror films, music was often played live by an orchestra or pianist, as film soundtracks did not yet exist. The first soundtracks were recorded in 1927, but it wasn't until the 1930s that music became an important element in horror films. Composers began creating musical themes for horror films, such as the famous scores for «Frankenstein» (1931) and «Dracula» (1931). Bernard Herrmann's music for «Psycho» (1960) became one of the most famous and iconic scores in the history of horror cinema.

Over the years, directors have experimented with different musical styles to accompany horror films. Some have used classical or symphonic music, while others have used more modern genres such as rock or electronic music. John Carpenter's music for «Halloween» (1978) is an example of synthetic music that has left a mark on the history of horror cinema. It has influenced many other horror films from the 1980s.

Sound effects are also crucial in creating a terrifying atmosphere in horror films. Footsteps, creaking doors, and screams can heighten tension in suspenseful moments. Monster and creature sounds need to be realistic to bring these characters to life on screen. Modern horror films have also used sound effects to create immersive sound environments, such as in «It Follows» (2014) where music and ambient sounds create an eerie atmosphere.

Lastly, the way music and sound effects are used in editing and narrative rhythm can have a major impact on the final result. Sound can be used to create smooth transitions between scenes or to create abrupt and shocking cuts. Directors can also use music to unsettle the viewer, using unexpected sound patterns or incorporating discordant sounds to generate tension.

Editing and Narrative Rhythm

Editing and narrative rhythm are key elements of horror cinema that create an immersive and frightening cinematic experience for the audience. These techniques are used to manipulate the viewer's emotions, creating moments of tension, suspense, terror, and catharsis.

Editing involves assembling different shots and sequences of a film to create a coherent and fluid story. In horror cinema, editing is used to create unexpected transitions, surprise effects, and to show the unseen. Directors can use fast editing to depict violent scenes or create a sense of panic, while slow editing can be used to create an oppressive atmosphere and a sense of anticipation.

Narrative rhythm is also an important element in creating a frightening ambiance. It refers to the tempo and timing of the story's progression, which can vary from slow and calm to fast and chaotic. A slow rhythm can be used to create a sense of unease and suspense, while a fast rhythm can be used to create a sense of chaos and panic.

In horror cinema, editing and narrative rhythm are used to gradually reveal horror. Directors can use these techniques to show the tension and fear experienced by the characters. For example, in the film «The Babadook,» director Jennifer Kent uses a slow rhythm to gradually reveal the monster haunting the main character, Amelia. This slow rhythm allows the audience to feel the same fear and terror as the main character.

Directors can also use editing and narrative rhythm to create moments of catharsis and redemption in horror cinema. For example, in the film «Get Out,» director Jordan Peele uses editing and narrative rhythm to create a horrifying climax followed by a moment of redemption and liberation.

In addition to creating a frightening atmosphere, editing and narrative rhythm can also evoke more complex and nuanced emotions. For example, in «The Silence of the Lambs,» director Jonathan Demme uses tight editing to create an oppressive atmosphere and a slow rhythm to allow the audience to feel the anxiety of the main character, Clarice Starling. He also employs a fast and chaotic rhythm to depict moments of violence.

Horror Cinema Around the World

American Horror Cinema

American horror cinema is one of the most popular, influential, and profitable genres in the American film industry. From the early silent horror films to the present day, American filmmakers have created some of the scariest, most memorable, and iconic films of the genre.

One of the reasons for the success of American horror cinema is the ability of its filmmakers to capture the fears and anxieties of American society at a given time. They have managed to create films that resonate with and frighten audiences, using themes and motifs that echo collective fears.

For example, in the 1950s, American horror films portrayed atomic monsters and aliens, reflecting the fear of the Cold War and nuclear threat. In the 1970s, American horror films were marked by social and political critique, exploring themes such as corruption, urban violence, and the energy crisis.

Among the most famous filmmakers in American horror cinema is George A. Romero, who revolutionized the genre with his cult film «Night of the Living Dead» in 1968. Romero used zombies as a metaphor to criticize American society at the time, addressing themes such as racism and institutional violence. The film also became a symbol of counterculture and inspired many independent horror filmmakers.

Another influential director is John Carpenter, who created classics such as «Halloween» in 1978 and «The Thing» in 1982, defining the subgenres of slasher and psychological horror. «Halloween,» in particular, is considered one of the most influential films in the genre, popularizing the themes of serial killers and survival horror.

Since the 2000s, American horror cinema has experienced a resurgence with films like «Saw» (2004), «Hostel» (2005), and «Paranormal Activity» (2007). These films have emphasized gore and realism, exploring themes such as torture, violence, and psychological horror. They have also popularized the found footage narrative style, which simulates a subjective camera to give viewers the impression of experiencing the horror alongside the characters.

American horror cinema has also produced many successful franchises, such as «Friday the 13th,» «Freddy Krueger,» and «Scream,» as well as numerous remakes and reboots. However, this has also led to some fatigue and market saturation, prompting filmmakers to seek new approaches to the genre.

British Horror Cinema

British horror cinema has a rich history and has produced some of the most iconic films of the genre. It has often been associated with ghost stories and gothic atmosphere, but it has also explored other themes and subgenres.

The 1950s saw the peak of British horror cinema, with films

like «Village of the Damned» and «The Giant Behemoth» captivating audiences. However, it was in the 1960s that the genre truly took off with films like Georges Franju's «Eyes Without a Face» and Terence Fisher's «The Brides of Dracula,» which established a style and aesthetic for British horror cinema.

One of the most influential directors of this period was Hammer Film Productions, which produced a series of gothic horror films in the 1960s and 1970s. These films, such as «Horror of Dracula» and «The Curse of Frankenstein,» were often adaptations of classic horror literature, featuring actors like Peter Cushing and Christopher Lee who became genre icons.

In the 1970s, British horror cinema evolved into subgenres like the slasher with films like Terence Fisher's «The Hound of the Baskervilles» and Robin Hardy's «The Wicker Man.» These films emphasized a darker and more brutal aesthetic while maintaining the gothic atmosphere characteristic of British horror cinema.

In the following decades, British horror cinema continued to evolve and explore new subgenres such as body horror with David Cronenberg's «Naked Lunch» and Clive Barker's «Hellraiser.» It also continued to produce gothic horror films like Alejandro Amenábar's «The Others,» which received critical acclaim and resonated with audiences.

British horror cinema has also influenced other arts and media, such as music and television. Rock bands like Black Sabbath and Iron Maiden drew inspiration from British horror films, while TV shows like «Doctor Who» incorporated elements of the genre into their storytelling.

Asian Horror Cinema

Asian horror cinema has been one of the most innovative and captivating genres in recent decades. Asian horror films often have a unique and original approach that sets them apart from their Western counterparts. In this section, we will explore the characteristics of Asian horror cinema and its impact on the history of the genre.

Japan is one of the most well-known Asian countries for its horror cinema. J-Horror (Japanese horror) emerged in the 1990s with films like «Ring» (1998), «Ju-On: The Grudge» (2002), and «Dark Water» (2002). These films achieved great success worldwide and were often adapted for American cinema.

Japanese style is often characterized by the use of nightmarish imagery, non-linear storytelling, and a frightening soundtrack. Additionally, Japanese themes often involve spirituality and superstition, such as vengeful ghosts and malevolent spirits. For example, Masaki Kobayashi's «Kwaidan» (1964) is an anthology film featuring four ghost stories based on Japanese legends. The film is a true work of art, with stunning visuals and a haunting, poetic atmosphere.

South Korean horror cinema is also very popular. The South Korean style is often characterized by graphic violence and shocking content. South Korean horror films often explore intense psychological themes such as madness, revenge, and guilt. Films like «Oldboy» (2003) and «I Saw the Devil» (2010) have achieved great success internationally.

Director Kim Jee-woon is a master of horror cinema, and his film «A Tale of Two Sisters» (2003) is considered one of the best Asian horror films of all time. The film tells the story of two sisters who return to their family home after being hospitalized in a psychiatric institution. The film uses non-linear storytelling and a strange visual aesthetic to create an eerie atmosphere.

China has also produced horror films that gained international attention. Chinese horror cinema often incorporates local folklore and legends into its horror stories. Themes often include mythical creatures like ghosts, vampires, and malevolent spirits.

The Chinese film «The Eye» (2002) by Hong Kong directors the Pang Brothers is an example of a successful Chinese horror film. The film follows the story of a young woman who undergoes a cornea transplant and begins to see strange things. The film uses a psychological approach to create a tense atmosphere.

Asian horror cinema is also known for its innovative use of visual aesthetics. Films often utilize stylized images and vibrant colors to create a nightmarish atmosphere. Asian filmmakers are also known for their skillful use of camera work and staging, which create moments of dramatic tension.

For example, Japanese director Takashi Miike is known for his horror films that are both shocking and aesthetically fascinating. His film «Audition» (1999) follows the story of a widowed man who holds auditions to find a new wife. The film uses slow pacing and sumptuous visual aesthetics to create a tense and suspenseful atmosphere.

Asian horror cinema is also known for its dark and intense themes, which can reflect cultural fears and anxieties. For example, the Korean film «The Host» (2006) by director Bong Joon-ho explores fears related to pollution and environmental contamination. The film follows the story of a family who must save their daughter kidnapped by a monstrous creature that emerges from a polluted river.

In addition to their distinctive themes and aesthetics, Asian horror films have also influenced global horror cinema. American remakes of Asian films like «The Ring» and «The Grudge» have been highly successful with Western audiences. Western directors, such as Guillermo del Toro, have also been influenced by Asian horror cinema.

European Horror Cinema and other National Traditions

European horror cinema, like other national traditions, has contributed to the richness and diversity of the genre. Each country has brought its own vision and style to horror cinema, using its own myths, beliefs, and fears. In this section, we will explore some of the most representative European countries and their contributions to the genre.

British horror cinema is one of the most important in Europe and has influenced many world-renowned directors. The 1960s and 1970s saw a wave of British horror films known as «Hammer Horror,» often featuring vampires, werewolves, and monsters. Iconic films of this period include «Dracula,» «Frankenstein,» and «The Curse of the Werewolf.» More recently, films like «Shaun of the Dead» and «28 Days Later» have revitalized the genre while maintaining the characteristic humor and violence of British horror cinema.

Italian horror cinema is also highly influential, with a distinctive visual style and themes often borrowed from gothic and opera. The 1960s and 1970s saw the emergence of many Italian horror films known as «giallo,» which are characterized by complex plots, violent scenes, and sophisticated aesthetics. Renowned directors such as Dario Argento and Mario Bava influenced many filmmakers worldwide. Films like «Suspiria,» «Deep Red,» and «Black Sabbath» are emblematic examples of Italian horror cinema.

French horror cinema is often associated with the movement of «cinéma de l'étrange,» which mixes horror, fantasy, and eroticism. The 1960s and 1970s saw the emergence of directors like Jean Rollin and Alain Robbe-Grillet, who explored themes such as death, madness, and sexuality in their films. More recently, films like «Martyrs» and «High Tension» have renewed the genre while maintaining the visual style and themes characteristic of French horror cinema.

German horror cinema is also influential, with films like «Nosferatu» and «The Cabinet of Dr. Caligari» that have influenced filmmakers worldwide. More recently, films like

«Goodnight Mommy» have been praised for their visual style and innovative storytelling, revitalizing the genre.

Other European countries, such as Spain, Sweden, and Belgium, have also made significant contributions to the genre. Spanish horror cinema is often associated with the «terrormiento» movement, which focuses on violence and madness. Films like «The Nameless» and «The Devil's Backbone» are emblematic examples of this style. Swedish horror cinema is often associated with psychological horror films like «Let the Right One In» and «Border,» which explore themes of identity, marginalization, and difference. Lastly, Belgian horror cinema is often associated with experimental and arty horror films like «Calvaire» and «Amer,» which emphasize visual style and eerie atmosphere.

Reception and Criticism of Horror Cinema

The reception of the public and censorship

The reception of the public and censorship in horror cinema are key aspects to consider in the analysis of the genre. Since its beginnings, horror cinema has elicited mixed reactions from the public and critics. On one hand, some viewers are fascinated by the special effects, tense scenes, and fear provoked by horror films. On the other hand, others may be shocked or offended by the graphic violence, explicit sexuality, vulgar language, and depictions of death and blood.

Censorship has been a constant concern for horror filmmakers, as horror films have often been associated with controversial or subversive themes. Censors have frequently imposed restrictions on violence, sexuality, and language, and have sometimes outright banned certain horror films. Filmmakers have circumvented these restrictions by using tricks such as suggestion rather than explicit representation of violence, or by modifying the content of films to make them more acceptable.

The public has also played a significant role in the reception of horror cinema. Filmmakers often target specific audiences, such as teenagers or horror film enthusiasts, using targeted marketing techniques. The commercial success of horror films has been fueled by a passionate fan base that has propelled horror film franchises like «Halloween» and «Friday the 13th» into popular culture.

However, some critics have also highlighted the artistic potential of the genre and have showcased horror films that are considered cinematic masterpieces, such as Roman Polanski's «Rosemary's Baby» or Stanley Kubrick's «The Shining». These films have explored deeper themes such as human psychology, paranoia, and madness and have been hailed for their aesthetics and their ability to provoke thought in the viewer.

The reception of the public and censorship have also evolved over time. In the 1970s and 1980s, the slasher genre experienced growing popularity, with films like «Halloween» and «Friday the 13th» being enthusiastically received by teenagers and young adults. However, these films also sparked controversy due to their graphic violence and depictions of women as victims.

More recently, horror cinema has experienced a revival with films like «Get Out» and «Hereditary» which have been acclaimed by critics and audiences for their originality and their ability to transcend genre boundaries. These films have explored contemporary social and political themes such as racism and dysfunctional families, using horror elements to heighten the emotional impact on the viewer.

Criticism and theories about the genre

Horror cinema is a film genre that often elicits strong and passionate reactions from critics and film theorists. Since its origins, this genre has been criticized for its use of graphic violence and visceral horror. Some film theorists consider this representation of violence and human suffering morally reprehensible and believe that it can contribute to desensitizing the audience to real-life violence. Others, on the contrary, argue that horror cinema can have a cathartic function by allowing viewers to experience their fears and anxieties in a controlled and symbolic manner.

However, the criticisms aimed at horror cinema are not limited to its use of graphic violence. The genre is also accused of perpetuating stereotypes and negative portrayals of certain social groups, such as women, racial or ethnic minorities, or LGBTQ+ individuals. Some critics assert that the genre can reinforce prejudices and discrimination by associating certain characters with violent or deviant behavior.

Despite these criticisms, horror cinema continues to be a popular and influential film genre. Film theorists are interested in how the genre can subvert these stereotypes and challenge established social norms. Many horror films feature strong and independent female characters or minorities who defy social conventions. These characters can be seen as symbols of resistance against domination and oppression.

Horror cinema can also be studied from an aesthetic and technical standpoint. Film theorists often explore the use of colors, lighting, music, and special effects to create an atmosphere of unease and terror. They also examine how directors play with audience expectations to evoke emotional reactions. Horror cinema is a genre that lends itself particularly well to experimentation and formal innovation, making it a fascinating subject of study for film theorists.

Lastly, horror cinema can be read from a social and cultural perspective. Horror films often reflect the fears and anxieties of the society in which they are produced. They can also be used to comment on and critique social and political issues of their time. For example, zombie films can be interpreted as reflections on the fears associated with the HIV/AIDS epidemic in the 1980s and 1990s.

Awards and dedicated festivals

The section on awards and dedicated festivals in the book offers an opportunity to highlight the importance of these events for horror cinema. Indeed, dedicated festivals serve as meeting places for film professionals, fans, and critics, and they provide a platform to discover and showcase the best films of the genre.

Dedicated festivals for horror cinema are numerous worldwide, and they offer filmmakers, actors, and producers the opportunity to present their works to the public and industry professionals. They represent a privileged moment for horror film professionals to meet, share their passion, discuss the latest trends, and discover new talents.

Among the most well-known festivals, the International Fantastic Film Festival of Gérardmer in France, the Fantasia International Film Festival in Montreal, FrightFest in London, and the Screamfest Horror Film Festival in Los Angeles can be mentioned. Each festival has its own characteristics and showcases different films and directors, creating a great diversity in the presentation of horror cinema.

Dedicated festivals reward the best films of the genre with prestigious prizes such as the Grand Jury Prize or the Audience Award. These awards are an important recognition for filmmakers and can help in the distribution of their films to cinemas. They also represent an opportunity for independent films to gain increased visibility and be discovered by new audiences.

In addition to dedicated festivals, awards for horror films are also given at more general award ceremonies such as the Oscars or the Golden Globes. Although horror cinema is not often rewarded at these major ceremonies, some films have managed to win prestigious awards. For example, Jonathan Demme's «The Silence of the Lambs» won five Oscars in 1992, including Best Film, Best Director, Best Actor, and Best Actress.

In addition to awards and festivals, critics also play an important role in the recognition of horror cinema. Critics specialized in the genre have a significant impact on how films are received by the public and can help promote new talents and independent films. Specialized magazines such as Fangoria or Rue Morgue, as well as dedicated websites like Bloody Disgusting or Dread Central, have become indispensable sources for horror film fans.

Horror Cinema and Pop Culture

Franchises and Remakes

Franchises and remakes are significant aspects of modern horror cinema. A franchise is a series of films that share a common universe and characters, while a remake is a new version of an existing film. These two concepts are often intertwined, as franchises often have remakes or reboots to reintroduce characters and stories to a new generation.

Franchises are popular because they allow studios to capitalize on the success of a film by producing sequels that offer fans new adventures with familiar and beloved characters. The most famous horror franchises include «Halloween,» «Friday the 13th,» «A Nightmare on Elm Street,» and «Saw.» These franchises have produced numerous films that have been embraced by genre fans, but have also received mixed reviews from critics.

Remakes, on the other hand, are often controversial as they can be seen as pale copies of beloved original films. However, some horror remakes have been acclaimed by critics and have even surpassed the originals in terms of commercial success and cinematic quality. A notable example is David Cronenberg's «The Fly,» which has been hailed as a modern horror masterpiece.

However, remakes and franchises are not solely produced for profit. They can also provide an opportunity to revisit classic stories and characters with a modern perspective, exploring new ideas and adapting stories for contemporary audiences. Additionally, remakes can bring technical and cinematic improvements to original films, thanks to technological advancements and the expertise of modern filmmakers.

Finally, it is important to note that franchises and remakes are not exclusive to horror cinema, but are also present in other film genres. However, horror cinema is particularly suited to these concepts, as it often revolves around iconic stories and characters that can be revisited and reinvented for future generations.

Merchandising and Derivative Products

The popularity of horror cinema has spawned a multitude of derivative products and merchandise. Fans of the genre can find all kinds of items, from clothing to toys, food products, video games, and books.

Derivative products allow fans to showcase their love for horror cinema by wearing t-shirts featuring their favorite characters, decorating their homes with film posters, or collecting figurines of their beloved monsters. Brands have also recognized the importance of pop culture and the enthusiasm for horror films, creating exclusive product ranges.

Horror films have also inspired video games, theme park attractions, and escape games, allowing fans to immerse themselves in experiences related to their favorite films. Horror video games are particularly popular, with titles such as «Resident Evil,» «Silent Hill,» and «Outlast.»

Merchandising is also a way for film studios to generate additional revenue. Derivative products are often marketed alongside film releases, allowing fans to prolong their cinematic experience. Successful franchises such as «Halloween,» «Scream,» and «Saw» have generated millions of dollars through the sale of merchandise.

However, merchandising can also harm the artistic credibility of horror cinema. Derivative products are often targeted at a younger audience, which can give a negative and infantilizing image to the genre. Brands often seek to exploit the popularity of horror cinema by creating irrelevant and low-quality products.

Influences on Other Arts and Media

One of the most fascinating aspects of horror cinema is its ability to influence other arts and media. Since the inception of horror cinema, filmmakers have been inspired by previous written and visual works of fiction, such as gothic novels, fairy tales, illustrations, and paintings. However, horror cinema has also had a significant impact on other art forms, including literature, comics, music, video games, and television.

Literature is an area where horror cinema has had a considerable influence. Works by great authors such as Edgar Allan Poe, Bram Stoker, and H.P. Lovecraft have been adapted for film, breathing new life into their tales of terror. In turn, horror films have also inspired many fiction writers to create novels and stories of terror, such as Stephen King, Dean Koontz, and Anne Rice.

Similarly, comics have also been heavily influenced by horror cinema. Horror comics, such as «Tales from the Crypt,» emerged in the 1950s and have since been adapted into many other forms, including television shows and films. Iconic characters such as Freddy Krueger, Jason Voorhees, and Michael Myers have also appeared in comics.

Music is another area where horror cinema has left its mark. Soundtracks of horror films are often as chilling and memorable as the images that accompany them, and music composers have often been inspired by the genre. Many rock and metal bands, such as Alice Cooper and Marilyn Manson, have also been influenced by horror cinema, incorporating spooky and macabre elements into their music and stage performances.

Video games are another field where horror cinema has had a significant influence. Horror video games, such as Resident Evil and Silent Hill, have become extremely popular and have been widely inspired by horror films. Video games have also allowed players to experience terrifying encounters interactively, adding a new dimension to the horror genre.

Lastly, horror cinema has also made an impact on television. Horror television shows, such as «The Twilight Zone» and «The X-Files,» have been greatly influenced by horror cinema. Additionally, many television series have also been adapted from horror films, such as «Hannibal» and «Bates Motel.»

Future Perspectives

Current and Emerging Trends

The current and emerging trends in horror cinema are numerous and reflect the evolution of society and technology. Firstly, independent horror cinema has been booming in recent years. Independent filmmakers are able to express themselves with more creative freedom and offer more original and risky films than Hollywood productions. The modest budgets of these films are often compensated by innovative scripts and bold artistic approaches.

However, this trend is not limited to the United States, but is also observed worldwide. For example, French horror cinema is currently experiencing a successful period thanks to productions like Julia Ducournau's «Raw», which has won numerous international awards. Similarly, South Korean horror cinema has undergone a revival in recent years with films like «The Wailing» or «The Host».

At the same time, social and political horror films are gaining popularity, particularly by addressing themes such as feminism, racism, environmental issues, and mental health problems. These films show a greater awareness of contemporary issues and seek to raise public awareness. A notable example is Jordan Peele's film «Get Out», which has been praised for its portrayal of the reality of African Americans in the United States.

Found footage, popularized by films such as «The Blair Witch

Project» or «Paranormal Activity», is also an emerging trend in the horror genre. This filming technique gives the impression that the viewer is witnessing the events unfolding on the screen, thus enhancing immersion and creating realistic tension.

Foreign horror cinema continues to have a strong presence on the global stage, with countries like Japan, South Korea, and Spain producing innovative and high-quality films. Foreign directors often bring a different perspective to the classic themes and motifs of horror, broadening the horizons of viewers. For example, the Korean film «Train to Busan» was praised for its successful combination of horror and action, as well as its convincing representation of Korean society.

Finally, virtual reality and new technologies offer new opportunities for horror cinema. Immersive experiences such as escape rooms or horror video games allow viewers to experience terrifying situations in real-time. Horror cinema in virtual reality is also developing, offering even greater immersion in the horror universe. Films like «The Ring VR» or «Don't Knock Twice VR» provide horrifying virtual reality experiences that allow viewers to immerse themselves in terrifying worlds and interact with characters and events.

Additionally, the COVID-19 pandemic has also had an impact on horror cinema, with films exploring fears related to disease and quarantine. Films such as «Host», filmed during lockdown, or «Songbird», which imagines a pandemic lasting several years, have been created in response to this situation.

The Role of New Technologies and Streaming Platforms

Horror cinema has always been a genre that has evolved and adapted to new technologies and audience consumption habits. Recent technological advancements have brought new tools and production methods for horror filmmakers, enabling the creation of high-quality films on limited budgets. Furthermore, streaming platforms have offered a new way to watch horror films, allowing viewers to watch them anytime, anywhere, and on different devices.

The digital revolution has also opened up new possibilities for horror cinema. Practical techniques such as special effects, makeup, and costumes have been replaced by digital techniques, resulting in a loss of authenticity and visual impact in horror films. Horror filmmakers are now faced with a new challenge of combining digital and practical techniques to create an authentic and immersive visual experience for the audience.

However, new technologies have also allowed for the exploration of a wider range of subjects in the horror genre. Horror films now have the opportunity to address social and political issues such as climate change, immigration, economic inequalities, and social justice. Horror films can offer relevant social commentary while creating a memorable horror experience.

Streaming platforms have also had a significant impact on the future of horror cinema. Platforms such as Netflix, Hulu, Amazon Prime Video, and Shudder have fostered diversity in terms of subjects and styles within the horror genre, allowing independent filmmakers to showcase their films to a wider audience. Streaming platforms have also provided unprecedented visibility to international horror films, allowing viewers to discover horror films from different cultures and countries.

However, the proliferation of streaming platforms has also created an overload of horror films of varying quality, making it difficult for the audience to find superior quality films. To remedy this, streaming platforms can integrate AI-based recommendation tools, using algorithms to suggest horror films similar to those that viewers have enjoyed in the past.

Ultimately, the future of horror cinema will depend on filmmakers' ability to adapt to new technologies while maintaining the authenticity and visual impact of horror films. Creativity and innovation will be essential to create unique and captivating stories that capture the audience's interest.

Independent Horror Cinema and Promising Filmmakers

Independent horror cinema is a growing movement that brings together talented and innovative filmmakers. Unlike big Hollywood productions, these films are often produced on very limited budgets, yet they manage to captivate a loyal audience and achieve critical success.

These filmmakers have an entrepreneurial spirit and great creativity that allow them to make bold choices and push the boundaries of the genre. They are often driven by a passion for horror cinema and a desire to offer original stories and strong characters.

Among the promising filmmakers in independent horror cinema are Ari Aster, who directed the films «Hereditary» and «Midsommar», and Jordan Peele, with the films «Get Out» and «Us». These filmmakers have managed to offer innovative films that have appealed to a wide audience and have been praised by critics.

Independent horror cinema also provides a platform for female directors, who often struggle to find their place in the film industry. Women like Ana Lily Amirpour, with her film «A Girl Walks Home Alone at Night», or Jennifer Kent, with «The Babadook», have managed to impose their vision and style in an industry often dominated by men.

Independent horror cinema also offers an opportunity for lesser-known actors and actresses to shine in roles that allow them to showcase their talent. Films like «The Witch» by Robert Eggers, or «It Follows» by David Robert Mitchell, have launched the careers of talented young actors and actresses.

Finally, independent horror cinema is a means of discovering different stories and cultures. Films like «Tigers Are Not Afraid» by Issa López, or «Train to Busan» by Yeon Sang-ho, offer original visions of the genre, allowing viewers to discover fascinating and often overlooked universes.

Social and Political Horror: Reflecting Contemporary Issues

Horror cinema has often been seen as an entertaining genre, designed to provoke fear and anxiety in the audience. However, the social and political implications of this genre should not be underestimated. Indeed, horror can reflect contemporary issues in our society and address important themes such as sexism, racism, discrimination, and police violence.

Horror cinema can thus become a form of social and political criticism, denouncing unjust and oppressive situations. For example, Jordan Peele's film «Get Out» made in 2017 addresses the issue of latent racism in contemporary American society. The film depicts a young African American man invited to his white girlfriend's family, where he is confronted with a series of racist and oppressive behaviors. The film uses the codes of horror cinema to denounce the mechanisms of racism and white dominance.

Similarly, James DeMonaco's film «The Purge» in 2013 imagines a dystopian America where, once a year, all crimes are legalized for one night. Behind this horrific premise, the film tackles crucial social and political issues such as violence, economic inequalities, and power dynamics between social classes.

Horror cinema can also address more specific issues, such as violence against women. Coralie Fargeat's film «Revenge» in 2017 tells the story of a young woman who is raped and left for dead in the desert, and who embarks on a bloody vendetta against her attackers. The film uses the codes of horror cinema to denounce sexist violence and the mechanisms of patriarchal oppression.

Finally, horror cinema can be a source of emancipation and resistance for oppressed minorities. Jennifer Kent's film «The Babadook» in 2014 portrays a single mother raising her autistic son and confronted with a monster from a children's book. The film can be read as an allegory for the fight against homophobia and social marginalization, with the main character being a lesbian mother facing a hostile and discriminatory society.

Challenges and Opportunities for the Future of the Genre

Horror cinema is a genre that has evolved over the decades, but it must continue to reinvent itself to remain relevant. To do so, it must face certain challenges and seize certain opportunities to ensure its future.

One of the main challenges for horror cinema is to maintain a high level of quality in its productions. With the expansion of the horror market, an increasing number of films are released every year, making it difficult to distinguish between high-quality productions and mediocre films. This can lead to market saturation and a loss of interest from the audience for the genre. To avoid this, filmmakers must demonstrate originality in their stories, creativity in their visual approach, and technical expertise to ensure a high-quality cinematic experience.

Another challenge is to maintain fear as a central element of the genre. Horror films must continue to explore unsettling themes and create atmospheres that evoke strong emotions in viewers. This can be difficult to achieve with market saturation, the availability of information, and desensitization to shocking and violent scenes. Filmmakers must therefore be aware of the importance of fear in horror cinema and strive to provoke it using creative and innovative techniques.

A third challenge for the genre is to meet the demands of new generations of viewers. Younger generations have different expectations when it comes to horror cinema, and it is important for the genre to be able to adapt to these new expectations to remain relevant. Filmmakers must therefore listen to the tastes and preferences of the audience and be able to adapt to new technologies and streaming platforms to reach new audiences.

Despite these challenges, horror cinema also presents many opportunities for the future. One of the most important is the expansion of the horror film industry worldwide. Horror film productions are no longer limited to major American studios but are increasingly being created in other countries, including Asia, Europe, and Latin America. This allows for the discovery of new stories, new directing styles, and new talents.

Another opportunity for horror cinema is the possibility to engage with social and political themes. Horror cinema can be an excellent way to explore the problems of our society, such as inequalities, discrimination, or the ecological crisis. By addressing these subjects, filmmakers can create relevant and engaging stories that resonate with audiences on a deeper level than just fear.

Finally, horror cinema can also benefit from the emergence of new technologies such as virtual reality and augmented reality. These technologies offer the possibility to create immersive cinematic experiences that can intensify fear and anxiety in viewers. Filmmakers can also use these technologies to experiment with new narrative forms and visual techniques that can transform the horror genre.

Conclusion

Horror Cinema: an Ever-Evolving Genre

Horror cinema is a constantly evolving film genre, constantly adapting to the tastes and expectations of the audience. Since its inception, it has undergone numerous transformations, both in terms of aesthetics and narrative. Today, horror cinema is more diverse than ever, with a multitude of sub-genres and different styles coexisting and blending together.

Some of the most notable evolutions in horror cinema are undoubtedly linked to technological advances and changing social mores. The 1960s and 1970s, for example, witnessed the emergence of a new type of horror cinema, more subversive and violent than films from previous decades. Movies such as George A. Romero's «Night of the Living Dead» or Tobe Hooper's «The Texas Chain Saw Massacre» disrupted the conventions of the genre by offering darker and more complex stories, where violence was often explicit and graphic.

In the 1980s and 1990s, horror cinema turned to slashers and psychological horror. Films like John Carpenter's «Halloween» or Wes Craven's «A Nightmare on Elm Street» popularized the masked killer archetype and introduced a new type of fear, more insidious and psychological, where the threat is often unseen and unpredictable.

More recently, horror cinema has experienced a true

resurgence with the arrival of new directors and sub-genres. Independent horror films such as Robert Eggers' «The Witch» or Ari Aster's «Hereditary» breathed new life into the genre by offering more intimate and personal stories, where fear is often intertwined with social or familial issues. Other sub-genres, such as found footage or survival horror, have also gained increasing success in recent years, exploring new narrative and aesthetic techniques.

Despite these evolutions, horror cinema remains a challenging genre to define, often associated with clichés and stereotypes. However, it is now recognized as a genre in its own right, with its own codes, conventions, and masterpieces. More than just entertainment, horror cinema is also fertile ground for reflection on the fears and anxieties of our time, and how they are represented on screen.

The Importance of Horror Cinema's Cultural and Artistic Heritage

Horror cinema is a film genre that holds a significant place in our cultural and artistic heritage. Since its inception, it has been considered a minor and controversial sub-genre, but over time, it has become an important film genre that has influenced many other genres.

The importance of horror cinema's cultural and artistic heritage lies in the fact that it has been a catalyst for many technical and narrative advances in cinema as a whole. Horror film directors have often used avant-garde techniques such as fast editing, sound, special effects, and makeup to create an immersive experience for the audience.

Horror cinema has also been a means for filmmakers to address important social and political issues. Horror films have often been used to tackle subjects such as sexism, racism, domestic violence, war, and economic exploitation. Many horror films have also addressed issues of mental health, addiction, and trauma, opening up important conversations on these topics.

In addition to this, horror cinema has influenced many other film genres, such as action films, thrillers, and dramas. The themes and techniques used in horror films have been adapted to other genres, creating more complex and immersive films.

Furthermore, horror cinema has had a significant impact on popular culture. Horror films often inspire artists, writers, musicians, and game creators. The monsters and iconic characters from horror films have become icons of popular culture, reinforcing the cultural heritage of the genre.

Finally, horror cinema is important because it allows us to explore our deepest and most primal fears. Horror films allow us to experience things we would never otherwise experience and confront our deepest fears and anxieties. This can help us better understand ourselves and the world around us.

In conclusion, horror cinema is an important film genre that has influenced many other genres, has created significant technical and narrative advancements, has addressed important social and political issues, has had a significant impact on popular culture, and allows us to confront our deepest fears. It is a cultural and artistic heritage that deserves to be recognized and celebrated.

Selective Filmography of Horror Cinema

The filmography of horror cinema is vast and covers a wide variety of films. Horror films have always been popular with the audience, and their history dates back over a century. Over the years, many horror films have become classics and have influenced many directors.

It is important to note that the list of films presented here is a subjective and non-exhaustive selection. It does not claim to be the ultimate list of horror films, but rather a compilation of films that have had significant impact on the genre and have contributed to shaping its evolution.

«Nosferatu» (1922) - Directed by F.W. Murnau, this is one of the first horror films in the history of cinema. It is inspired by Bram Stoker's novel «Dracula» and features the most famous vampire in history.

«Frankenstein» (1931) - Directed by James Whale, this film is an adaptation of Mary Shelley's novel of the same name. It portrays Dr. Frankenstein, who creates a creature made of different body parts. This film launched the career of Boris Karloff, who portrays the creature.

«Psycho» (1960) - Directed by Alfred Hitchcock, this film

revolutionized the horror genre by showing violence in a more explicit manner. It features a serial killer and created a psychological tension that captivated the audience.

«Night of the Living Dead» (1968) - Directed by George A. Romero, this is one of the most famous zombie films of all time. It portrays a group of people fighting to survive against hungry zombies.

«The Exorcist» (1973) - Directed by William Friedkin, this is one of the most controversial horror films of all time. It depicts a young girl possessed by a demon and elicited strong reactions from the audience and critics.

«Halloween» (1978) - Directed by John Carpenter, this film is considered one of the best slasher films of all time. It features Michael Myers, a serial killer who escapes from a psychiatric hospital and stalks his victims throughout the town.

«The Shining» (1980) - Directed by Stanley Kubrick, this film is based on Stephen King's novel and features Jack Nicholson as a caretaker of an isolated hotel who becomes deranged. The film creates an atmosphere of tension that unsettles the audience.

«A Nightmare on Elm Street» (1984) - Directed by Wes Craven, this film popularized the character of Freddy Krueger. He is a serial killer who attacks his victims in their dreams, creating terrifying nightmare scenes.

«Ring» (1998) - Directed by Hideo Nakata, this film is considered one of the best Japanese horror films of all time. It portrays a cursed videotape that kills those who watch it. The film sparked the wave of Asian ghost films and inspired many remakes.

«The Blair Witch Project» (1999) - Directed by Daniel Myrick and Eduardo Sánchez, this film popularized the found footage style, where the film is presented as a compilation of found videos after an event. The film follows three students who disappear in a haunted forest.

«Saw» (2004) - Directed by James Wan, this film is considered the beginning of a successful franchise. It features a serial killer who kidnaps his victims and subjects them to deadly trials.

«Get Out» (2017) - Directed by Jordan Peele, this film is a critique of American society and its racial issues. It portrays a young black man who meets his white girlfriend's family and discovers a disturbing secret.

«Hereditary» (2018) - Directed by Ari Aster, this film is considered one of the best horror films of the last decade. It depicts a family haunted by dark secrets after the grandmother's death.

«Us» (2019) - Directed by Jordan Peele, this film portrays a family that is attacked by sinister doppelgangers of themselves. The film explores themes of duality and human nature.

«Midsommar» (2019) - Directed by Ari Aster, this film takes place in an isolated Swedish community that celebrates an annual festival. The film explores themes of loss and self-discovery.

In the end, this selective filmography of horror cinema only scratches the surface of a rich and complex genre that has been constantly evolving for over a century. The films mentioned here have had a significant impact on the genre and have contributed to shaping its evolution. Fans of the genre will certainly find other films to add to this list based on their personal preferences.

Acknowledgments

In conclusion to this work, I would like to express my profound gratitude to all the individuals who have contributed, directly or indirectly, to the creation of «Screen Nightmares: Everything You Need to Know About the Depths of Horror Cinema».

First and foremost, I would like to warmly thank the experts and enthusiasts who have shared their knowledge and experience with me. Their generosity and enthusiasm have been valuable sources of inspiration to fuel my reflections and bring this work to life.

I would like to salute all the professionals in the horror cinema industry - directors, screenwriters, actors, technicians, and producers - whose talent and creativity have allowed this film genre to develop and constantly renew itself. Thanks to them, generations of viewers have been able to thrill, marvel, and reflect on human nature through these works of art.

My thanks also go to all the critics and academics who have contributed to enriching the reflection on horror cinema. Their work has been essential in giving meaning to this unique genre and in enlightening my understanding of its cultural and social issues.

Finally, I would like to express my gratitude to my loved ones - family and friends - for their unwavering support, patience, and encouragement. Their presence and understanding have been indispensable sources of motivation to successfully carry out this ambitious project.

Dear readers, as you close this book, I hope to have offered you a fascinating and enlightening journey through the rich universe of horror cinema. May these pages have inspired you to look at this film genre with fresh and curious eyes, and encourage you to explore further the treasures it holds.

Once again, thank you all, and enjoy your continued exploration of horror cinema!